Looking for Love in All the Wrong Places

by

Dina Jones

Bloomington, IN  Milton Keynes, UK

authorHOUSE®

AuthorHouse™
1663 Liberty Drive, Suite 200
Bloomington, IN 47403
www.authorhouse.com
Phone: 1-800-839-8640

AuthorHouse™ UK Ltd.
500 Avebury Boulevard
Central Milton Keynes, MK9 2BE
www.authorhouse.co.uk
Phone: 08001974150

First published by AuthorHouse 6/7/2007

ISBN: 978-1-4259-8504-2 (sc)

Library of Congress Control Number: 2007901621

Printed in the United States of America
Bloomington, Indiana

This book is printed on acid-free paper.

♥
♥

Dedication

*T*his book is dedicated to all women in the world who have endured abuse at the hands of someone. Whether it is a loved one, or a significant other, abuse of any kind is unacceptable. If you are in an abusive relationship, I urge you to seek professional counsel. The abuser will not change, so please don't stick around hoping he will. You are only in control of yourself, and if you change the things that are unacceptable to you, the abuser loses power. Trust in God because all things are possible with him. Most of all, please remember, no one can do anything to you that you don't allow them to. Be strong, love yourself and keep the faith. To my loving husband, children and mother thanks for being there for me. You are all the wind beneath my wings. Much love to you all. To my distinguished Pastor, it was your insightful preaching and teaching of the gospel of Jesus Christ that led me to Christ and helped me make the decision to leave the abusive relationship that I endured. I can't thank you enough for your powerful sermons. Last, but not least thanks and glory be to God. Because of his grace and mercy, I am alive today – alive to tell my story to help someone else in need. To God be the glory!!

CHAPTER I

I want to know what love is

Love is patient; love is kind; does not envy; love does not boast;
Love is not proud; Love is not rude; Love is not self-seeking; Love is
not easily angered;
Love keeps no records of wrongs; Love does not delight in evil;
but rejoices in truth; Love bears all things;
believes all things; hopes all things; endures all things;
Love never fails.

Corinthians: 13:4-8

Tawana and Jerome began dating in the summer of 1975. Although they lived next door to each other, on a block where everyone knew everyone else, and were next door neighbors, they never gave each other a second thought. For one, Jerome wasn't really Tawana's type. Tawana was a good girl in school and in general. Jerome was bad – bad to the bone. He was always fighting, getting suspended and everything. In spite of all the trouble that Jerome managed to get into, he began to take notice of Tawana. He would tell his sister Jasmine to hook them up, since Jasmine and Tawana hung out at times. Jasmine never took him seriously, but when she mentioned to Tawana that Jerome liked her, Tawana gave Jasmine her number and told her to have Jerome call her. Jerome was a cutie and all the girls in school were after him. Tawana got a kick out of the fact that the guy every one was after, was actually after her. About a month after they began dating, Jerome was arrested for burglary. Tawana was shocked when Jasmine told her, especially since Tawana had no idea that Jerome was that bad. They had already begun dating before he was arrested, and Tawana had really started liking him. She liked Jerome so much that she would sneak and go on visits with Jerome's mother. Tawana did not know before his arrest that Jerome was failing miserably in school. She on the other hand, was about to graduate from high school, waiting to begin her new job and was pretty much looking forward to life. Although Tawana and Jerome really had nothing in common, she was smitten by him. She knew that this relationship wasn't a good one from the start, but she was determined to make it work. Tawana sometimes thrived on Jerome's bad boy image, and although they were exact opposites, their relationship bloomed into something that Tawana had not expected. Besides the fact that he was very handsome, she didn't know other things about him that surely would put a different light on their relationship. The things that she didn't know about Jerome were the things that were certainly destined to ruin their relationship. She didn't know that he had a problem keeping his hands to himself or that he had a very short temper. She didn't know that he wanted her all to himself, he was very jealous natured. In hindsight, Tawana probably should've walked away from the relationship. The only thing is Jerome was smart. He was always on his best behavior when she visited him in prison. For one, if he had ever put his hands on her during a visit, his visits would've been stopped. Another reason why he hid his true self from Tawana was that he needed her support. He needed somebody to take care of him once he got out of prison until he got on his feet. Tawana didn't know this. She was smart, very smart. But she did not have the street smarts of a hustler. Jerome knew the streets – and he knew them well. Tawana was in for the ride of her life. She was about to go somewhere she'd never imagined – not even in her wildest dreams.

It was a sunny summer day in July, 1977 and Jerome had just walked out of the upstate prison a free man. Tawana was at home anxiously awaiting his arrival. She was so excited finishing the final touches of the party, making sure the house was in order and really looking forward to Jerome's homecoming. She had sent the invitations out months in advance once she knew that the parole board was releasing him from prison. Most of their friends responded that they would be attending because they were really excited to see Jerome come home and they also wanted to help Tawana celebrate since she had always been good to all of them. The menu Tawana had planned was awesome. Kobe steak, shrimp, lobster, different salads, some pasta, delicious pastries and cakes, and of course, top-shelf bubbly. Tawana had spent a lot of money on this party and she hoped that Jerome would at least appreciate it. She had no reason to believe otherwise. From the corner of her eye, Tawana spotted a shiny black Lincoln Continental limo driving up her block. Everything seemed to stop for that one magic moment. As the door to the limo opened, out stepped a 6'1" bald black man who looked damn good. Tawana was looking out of the window as the car approached her house. When she saw Jerome she could not believe how handsome he was. She wanted to jump out of the window right then and there. It had only been two years – although it seemed longer that Jerome was away, and although Tawana longed for a relationship, she remained faithful to Jerome. None of her friends could understand why Tawana remained faithful to Jerome, but they didn't dare question her decision. They already knew that Tawana was her own woman and when she made up her mind, there was really nothing anyone could do about it. As Jerome began walking up the stairs to Tawana's apartment, he looked up to the sky at the beautiful fluffy white clouds. The clouds looked so much different in the free world than they looked when he was incarcerated. Maybe it was all in his mind, but he was happy as hell to be a free man. He had a look on his face as if he had died and gone to heaven. Tawana was waiting at the door and all of their friends were huddled all over her apartment waiting for her to give the cue that Jerome was at the door. As she peered through the peephole she saw Jerome's smile change to a frown. He must've had an idea what was going on. By the look on his face, Tawana didn't think he was pleased. Anyway, she opened the door and everyone ran out screaming "Welcome home Jerome". Jerome's facial expression went from a puzzled look to a look of shock. He did not look as if he appreciated the surprise. Tawana noticed the smirk on his face and wondered if she did something wrong. Everyone starting approaching Jerome giving him hugs, kisses, handshakes and wishing him well. Thus the party began. The food was served, dessert was served and out came the open bar. As 'Aint No Stoppin Us Now' played in the background, Tawana proceeded to toast her man and everyone chimed in with the toast. The bubbly circulated the room a few times and before long, the dining room was filled with a few partiers who had too much to drink. Tawana had an old baby grand piano in her dining room and she didn't want it damaged so she made an announcement that the last song would be played. It was already 2:00 a.m. Everyone danced to what really turned out to be the last song which was Reunited by Peaches & Herb. Tawana proposed one last toast to Jerome and as fast as they could, everyone started leaving. It was about 3 a.m. by the time everyone said their goodbyes and Tawana was really tired. She decided she should start cleaning up so that she could sleep a little later the next day. She was almost finished washing the dishes when she looked over her shoulder and realized Jerome was standing there with a smirk on his face. Tawana grabbed a dish towel to dry her hands and then proceeded to walk over to where Jerome was standing. Before she could get to him, Jerome grabbed her arm in a very threatening manner and asked her "who the hell told you I wanted a surprise party?" Confused at his behavior, Tawana said, "I did it for you, I wanted to show you how much I loved you and decided having our friends over and throwing a party would be a good idea". Jerome looked at her as if he were scolding his naughty daughter and said to her "who told you to think, if I wanted a party I would've asked for one. I've just been released from prison, have no freaking clothes and here you are throwing me a damn party…woman are you out of your mind?" Tawana could not believe her ears. After all she had went through planning this party, Jerome could've at least been appreciative. Tawana looked at Jerome and said "you are a selfish bastard - I did this for you. "Why can't you appreciate it?". With that, Jerome turned around and back-handed Tawana so hard that she flew into the cherry wood wall unit in her dining room. Tawana got up wiped her bleeding lip and said to Jerome, "what the hell is wrong with you?" Jerome replied, the next time you want to throw a party for someone, maybe you should ask. "Surprise, Tawana shouted, that's why it's called a surprise – because you don't know about it." Jerome didn't hear her, he told her she'd better not plan another party without his knowledge and if she did it again, he'd slap her silly the next time. The next time, Tawana thought. What is he talking about? She had never experienced a man hitting her and she wasn't about to start now….at least that's what she thought.

It had only been a few months since Jerome was released from prison. Unfortunately, those few months began to take a toll on Tawana. Jerome wasn't working, wasn't looking for a job and the one and only job that he managed to get he got fired from. Apparently he lied about his criminal background and when his fingerprints came back, he was terminated by the company. Their rule for hiring was that you could have a criminal record and work as a security guard. They just didn't want you lying and saying you didn't have a criminal record and then they find out otherwise. So, Tawana began to feel trapped. Something had to give. She could not continue taking care of this grown man. She felt as if she were losing control over her life. It was an uneasy feeling especially since she was used to being in control of her life.

♥

♥

CHAPTER II

A Fool's Paradise

Trust in the Lord with all your heart,
and lean not on your own understanding;
in all your ways acknowledge Him,
and He shall direct your paths.

Proverbs 3:5

On her train ride to work every morning, Tawana began to wonder if this relationship was what she really wanted. She couldn't see things getting better anytime soon and she was afraid. She began to think of all the things that Jerome was taking away from her. He was literally draining her, but she was inclined to hold on and make it work. Meanwhile, Jerome was eating her out of house and home and his latest thing was smoking weed all day long. Tawana would leave him money to go job-hunting, he would buy weed instead. One day Tawana arrived home from work to find Jerome stretched out on her antique leather sofa. She went ballistic. "Get your ass up Jerome -you haven't paid for anything in here, you don't want to work and I'm tired of coming home and finding my house a mess". "Your house, oh, now it's your house, huh", Jerome replied. "It's always been my house Jerome. I just loved you enough to welcome you here with me. Unfortunately you don't seem to appreciate what I've done for you. You seem to be taken me for granted". The moment those words came out of her mouth, this paralyzing fear engulfed her entire body. Tawana never saw him coming, he picked her up off the floor and dropped her backwards. Her head hit the bottom of the microwave cart and she was in excruciating pain. She attempted to grab a chair to steady herself and get back on her feet, but Jerome stood right there and the minute she felt herself getting up, he took his foot and kicked her back down. Tawana sat there for a moment, immobilized by the pain. Jerome's hitting was becoming a bit too much for her. She could not get used to being with someone who couldn't keep his hands to himself. She began sobbing uncontrollably – she was in so much pain. Jerome could care less. He looked in the fridge, grabbed a beer and went in the living room to watch television. Tawana sat on the floor a little while longer. She grabbed on to the stool next to the island in the kitchen for balance. She made her way pass Jerome in the living room and went straight to the bathroom. Once in the bathroom, she looked in the mirror and just began to cry some more. She tried to control her sobs by putting her hand over her mouth but the pain was just too much to bear. Tawana decided to call her best friend Bethany. After Tawana told Bethany all about what Jerome had just done to her, Bethany was ready to come over and kick Jerome's ass, but Tawana remained calm and told Bethany that was not necessary – this was her problem to deal with. They talked for a while longer until Tawana told Bethany she was tired and was about to take a long hot bath and go to bed. Bethany asked Tawana if she was afraid to be in the house with Jerome and Tawana told her no, that she'd be okay. With that Bethany and Tawana hung up the phone and Tawana began to run her bath water. The heat felt so good on her skin that you could literally see steam coming from her skin. Tawana did not want to get out of the tub. The water caressed every inch of her body, and she really needed it. By the time Tawana was ready to get out of the tub, she was drained. She dried herself off, grabbed her robe from the back of the bathroom door, slid her feet into her slippers and made her way to the bedroom. To her delight, Jerome was still in the living room. He was fast asleep without a worry in the world. She slowly slid into her bed and tried to fall asleep. It was too hard. She stayed up thinking about Jerome and his temper and what her life had become. She could not believe that somebody could be so evil and unappreciative. Tawana said her prayers and laid there waiting to fall asleep. Twenty minutes later, she was snoring...without a care in the world.

♥

♥

CHAPTER III

The Sun will come out Tomorrow

Weeping may endure for a night,
but joy comes in the morning.

Psalms 30:5

The slither of sun that was peeking through the well hung drapes was blinding to Tawana and she began to awake. She sat up unable to believe what she smelled. Moments later Jerome entered the room apparently well-rested and greeted Tawana with a tray full of different foods. Jerome got up early this morning, went out to get all this food to cook and made his lady a beautiful breakfast complete with fruit and coffee. Tawana thought to herself this must be one of the benefits of incarceration – because that's where Jerome learned how to cook. Tawana was a bit surprised by this breakfast in bed scenario and could not find the right words to say after Jerome had placed everything down in front of her. But before she could utter a word Jerome had removed his apron, knelt down next to Tawana's side of the bed and began kissing her passionately. Tawana allowed herself to be lost in his embrace and at that moment she felt secure with him. Jerome then gently grabbed her face, looked into her eyes and told her he was sorry for his behavior lately. He explained to her that he was upset that he couldn't find a job since being released from prison and how he hated not being able to contribute to the household. Tawana told him that she understood and simply encouraged him to keep trying. Jerome agreed with Tawana. He hugged her and told her how much he loved her. Jerome then crawled into bed next to Tawana and began to caress her body all over. The food would have to wait. It had been two years since he had any type of contact with the opposite sex. Tawana was ready too. She let everything go and decided to go with the flow. She wanted to enjoy the moment no matter where it took her she just wanted to be loved.

♥
♥

CHAPTER IV

Three's a Crowd

Cast your burden (or cares) upon the Lord,
and He shall sustain you.

Psalm 55:22.

He had been released from prison four years earlier and Jerome was still having a problem holding a job. The unfortunate thing was that Tawana had just found out that she was pregnant. She was not happy at all. She wasn't sure if she even wanted a baby with Jerome. How could he take care of her and the baby when he could barely take care of himself? Tawana knew that she could not rely on Jerome to help her take care of a baby – but part of her wanted this baby so bad. Tawana felt that a baby would do her some good. It would give her something to focus on – something to love so to speak. After leaving the doctor's office, Tawana flagged down a cab for the ride home. She cried the entire ride. She contemplated whether she should tell Jerome and how he would react if she did tell him. Being the person she was, she felt it only right to tell him. When she arrived home she noticed the lights were on upstairs. It was only 7:30 in the evening, but she was hoping that Jerome was out in the street somewhere. She climbed the stairs slowly because she really didn't want to see Jerome right now. She had to digest the fact that she was pregnant, considering keeping the baby, and Jerome had no job. When she reached the top of the stairs she noticed the door to her apartment was open. Jerome was in the hall with a few friends and they were playing dice. Tawana could not believe her eyes but then again she was glad because she didn't have to tell him the news yet. She went inside the apartment to her bedroom and closed the drapes. She threw herself across her bed and began to cry. This wasn't your normal crying. Her body was trembling with pain because for the first time in her life Tawana really felt alone. She cried so hard that she cried herself to sleep. When Jerome did come into the apartment, it was dark and quiet. He went into the bedroom and saw Tawana stretched out across the bed still in her clothes. He wanted to wake her up but decided against it. Instead, he found her pocketbook in her closet and helped himself to some of her money. He slid her pocketbook back into her closet and went back into the living room. She must've had a long day he thought. He backed out of the room and went into the living room. A few minutes later, the thief was fast asleep.

It was about 1 o'clock in the morning and Tawana was awaken by the sound of cars drag racing down the street. She got up to go get some water and found Jerome in the living room watching television. After getting a glass of water, she went into the living and sat down next to Jerome. "Jerome, we need to talk." "Sure baby, sit down" he said, patting the space next to him. Tawana sat down and began telling Jerome that she was pregnant and not sure what to do. Job or not, Jerome was happy with the news. "Hold on Jerome, before you get all happy, I'm not sure whether I'm having this baby or not. I can't take care of a child by myself". "You don't have to, replied Jerome. I'm going to get a job Tee. Trust me when I tell you, I am". Tawana heard him, but what he said to her went in one ear and came out the next. She didn't believe one word of what he said. She would have to see this to believe it. They talked a little while longer and finally Tawana got up to go to bed. Jerome remained on the couch watching television for a while longer. Looks like tonight would be another night on the couch for Jerome.

The next morning when Tawana woke up she went straight to the kitchen past Jerome and started making some breakfast. She was really hungry this morning especially since she went to bed so early the night before without eating dinner. She made a plate for Jerome but covered it up and put it in the microwave so that he could eat his breakfast when he woke up. Tawana sat down and began to eat her breakfast. Her thoughts were swarming in her head, how was she going to take care of a baby by herself. Although Jerome promised that he would get a job, Tawana did not believe any of his promises. As the tears rolled down her face, Tawana wondered how she had gotten herself into this mess. She decided that her and Jerome needed to talk a little more than they had the night before. She would talk with Jerome when he woke up. She wanted to see what his plans were for this baby and if he had any intentions on getting a job.

It was noon time when Jerome finally got up. He couldn't believe that he slept this late and probably didn't remember any of their conversation the night before. When he got out of the shower, he went into the kitchen to get his breakfast. Jerome could tell something was bothering Tawana so he decided it was best to eat in the kitchen. After he finished his breakfast, he went into the living room and turned on the television. By this time, Tawana was fully dressed and ready to go run her errands. As she walked into the living room she saw Jerome on the couch flicking from channel to channel. A feeling of anger overcame Tawana and she wasn't sure whether she was angry because Jerome lived life so freer or because she was being a fool for him. Either way, she was about to let Jerome know exactly how she felt. Tawana sat down on the couch facing Jerome and began the conversation by asking Jerome what his plans were as far as what type of job he wanted. Jerome looked up at Tawana and began telling her how he had spoken with the dispatcher at a construction site and that he was waiting for them to get back to him. Tawana told Jerome to stop lying. She didn't believe one word of what he was saying. While the words were welcoming to Tawana's ears, Tawana always believed actions spoke louder than words – and judging by Jerome's actions, Tawana and the baby were in trouble. Jerome simply wasn't ready to grow up or become responsible. Tawana pushed at this point and asked Jerome when was the last time he went to see this dispatcher person. Jerome responded that he was just at the site last week and that the dispatcher told him to come back in a few weeks. The dispatcher supposedly told Jerome that the laborers are paid well and receive excellent benefits. Tawana didn't know whether Jerome was telling the truth, but again, she was willing to give him a chance to see for herself. She wasn't about to let Jerome know this so instead she told him that he needed to go back to the site and speak with the dispatcher as soon as possible. She told Jerome if he didn't get a job soon she was not keeping the baby and she was leaving him. As soon as the words came out of her mouth, Tawana saw a thick vein protruding from Jerome's forehead. Jerome got up off the couch walked over to Tawana who was now standing by the door on her way out, and said to her "did I ask you to take care of me, what the hell are you talking about?" Tawana was sick of Jerome's childish outbursts and decided she was going to stand her ground. After all she was pregnant and if Jerome hit her, she would have to call the police on him, whether he liked it or not. Tawana looked Jerome in the eyes and said to him "no, you didn't ask me to take care of you, but you don't seem to be in a rush to find a job either." With that, Jerome grabbed her cheeks, pulled her close to him as if she would have trouble hearing him and said "look woman, I did not ask you to take care of me, I told you I'll get a job, now get off of my back". They continued to argue and one thing led to another and the next thing they were fighting. Tawana knew she was no match for Jerome but she was truly sick of his behavior. Out the corner of her eye Tawana saw the broomstick, she ran to grab it and in seconds she was beating Jerome over the back with the broomstick. This made Jerome even angrier and he grabbed Tawana in a chokehold. Tawana proceeded to bite him on his arm. Instead of Jerome letting Tawana go, he pushed her to the floor. Tawana sat there for what seemed like days totally in disbelief. It seemed to her like this scene was becoming all too familiar. Although she feared for herself, her greatest fear at that moment was for her unborn child. Jerome's abuse was getting worse as time went by. Tawana had enough of his abusive behavior and this time she called 911. When the police officers arrived, they did the normal question and answer trying to figure out what happened. Tawana kept yelling to the officers that Jerome should be arrested since she is pregnant. The officers asked Jerome how long he had lived in the apartment. Jerome told the officers that they had been living together in the apartment for over 4 years and that he wasn't working. He also told the officer that he had no place to go. The officer looked at Tawana and said "Mam, I know this is your apartment but by law if this man has lived with you for over thirty days then he has a right to stay". Tawana could not believe her ears. How was that possible?

It was her apartment – and here she had to listen to an officer tell her that Jerome had a right to stay. Tawana looked at the officer and said, "I thought by law whenever someone hits a pregnant woman they can be arrested." The officer said that usually was the case, but they arrest people on a case by case basis. By this time Tawana could see a smirk on Jerome's face. Almost as if he were saying hah, I ain't going nowhere. The officer proceeded to tell Tawana that she could go to family court and get an order of protection against Jerome. Tawana thought what good was that – if the officer was standing there telling her that Jerome had a right to stay in her apartment, what good would it do to have an order of protection. Jerome had made it clear to the officer that he had no place to go. Tawana walked over to the officer and said "okay, I see how this is going but I'll tell you what, the next time you are called to this apartment you better bring a body bag because if he puts his hands on me again, I will kill him". The officer literally laughed in her face and proceeded to leave. His partner was in the bedroom talking to Jerome trying to tell him to calm down and that he should take a walk when he feels his temper getting out of control. Jerome pretended to be listening and Tawana knew once the officers left Jerome would start up all over again. To her surprise, after the officers left, Jerome sat down in the living room and began watching television. Maybe he felt as if he had wreaked enough havoc for one day. Tawana went to her bedroom and laid down. She would have to run her errands another day. Her head was spinning. Again, she thought, here I am thinking about something that should not have happened. She quietly wondered to herself when she would have enough of living like this – with an out of control abuser. No one knew the answer to that question but Tawana. Sadly, at the moment she didn't have an answer. All she knew was she was living the biggest lie in the world. The more he fought her, the more concerned her friends became. They even offered to help her with the baby for a while, they just wanted her to leave Jerome.

♥
♥

CHAPTER V

How do I love me, let me count the ways

Even if I dole out all that I have, and if I surrender my body
to be burned, but have not love
(God's love in me), I gain nothing.

Cor. 13:3

Over the course of the next few years Jerome's abusive behavior became worse. But by this time, Tawana was too scared to leave. She barely called the police on him and when she did call the police, she was too scared to press charges once they arrived. Tawana would tell her girlfriend Bethany that she was living the biggest lie of her life. Tawana and Bethany had been on the telephone for over two hours when Bethany realized that Tawana was crying. "What's the matter girl?" asked Bethany. After getting herself together Tawana told Bethany that she was living the biggest lie of her life. She told Bethany that when she's at work she's this happy go lucky person, but as soon as she reaches her front door, her whole demeanor changes. Tawana told Bethany that at times she would stand in the mirror and literally call herself a liar. Bethany was quiet for a while but then she said to Tawana "well being abused by someone is not something that you want to go around telling people". "No, that's not what I mean, Tawana responded. I won't even give myself enough credit to believe that I can leave him, Bethany. I'm so scared of him, that I just deal with it". No one else knew Tawana felt this way – only Bethany and Tawana was determined to keep it that way. Her mother had decided long ago to stay out of her relationship because she felt that Tawana was making the decisions she wanted to make. What her mother did not know was that Tawana was being abused by Jerome. Tawana was in a bad situation with Jerome. She could not understand why she wouldn't leave him. Jerome would make plans to go the movies or out to dinner and never had a dime to pay for anything. He made these plans with the full intention of spending Tawana's money. Jerome would call Tawana at work and say honey let's go out tonight and before Tawana could say yes or no, Jerome would say on your way home can you pick me up an outfit to wear. Tawana would think what nerve but she did it anyway. She was too afraid to tell Jerome no. Since Tawana was afraid to let anyone know what she was going through with Jerome she began writing in a diary. Every day she would write to God looking for answers. How could someone as smart as she not realize that being with Jerome was not a good thing for her. Not only was the situation bad for Tawana, now she was bringing another life into this situation. Things had gotten so out of control that Tawana couldn't even think straight.

♥
♥

CHAPTER VI

Friends, how many of us have them

Faithful are the wounds of a friend;
but the kisses of an enemy are deceitful.

Proverbs 27:6

It was the summer of 1980 and Tawana's best friend Bethany's house was the place to be. Bethany would make the biggest Sunday dinners which consisted of fried chicken, collards, macaroni and cheese. I mean the girl used to throw down. On this particular Sunday, Tawana felt like being alone, and she did not want Jerome to come with her to Bethany's house. Jerome stayed behind although he wasn't too happy about it. A few hours after Tawana left home, Bethany's bell rang. Jerome had followed Tawana to Bethany's house anyway. When he arrived Tawana and Bethany were sitting in the living room talking and playing cards. Jerome asked Tawana to come into the kitchen so he could talk to her. Bethany knew Jerome was up to no good so she watched from a mirror in her living room. She was able to see their shadows and then all of a sudden Bethany saw a frying pan full of grease go flying in her kitchen. Bethany was a neat freak so seeing this prompted her to run into the kitchen. When she got in the kitchen, Jerome was full of grease. Apparently Tawana had thrown the frying pan of grease on him and Bethany could see that he was really pissed off now. She told Tawana to go into the room and asked Jerome to leave. Bethany did not appreciate Jerome coming to her home and starting a fight with Tawana, especially since Tawana and Bethany were just shooting the breeze waiting for the food to get ready. They enjoyed their girl time which they didn't get much of these days. Jerome was so jealous that he made sure Tawana didn't see Bethany as much as she used to. As Jerome walked to the door to leave the apartment he turned around and punched Bethany in the face. Why did he do that, Tawana thought. Bethany grabbed the umbrella stand that was next to her door and commenced to whupping his ass with it. She hit him so hard that the umbrella stand broke over his back. Anybody else would've left and went about their business – but Jerome wasn't operating with a full deck of cards and as soon as Bethany thought things were clear, Jerome was banging on the door. He had called the police on Bethany. Bethany let the police in and began explaining to them what Jerome did in her apartment. The police told Bethany that she would have to go down to the stationhouse because Jerome was pressing charges against her. Bethany couldn't believe this shit. How the hell does he get to press charges against me, when he was the one fighting in my home? What's that about, Bethany asked the police. The police told Bethany that she should've knocked Jerome's ass out when he was actually in her apartment and not in the hallway. Just then Tawana interrupted and told the officer that it was Jerome who started the fight. She explained to the officers that she was visiting Bethany and Jerome just came over without being invited. She told them how he had mushed her in the face and how she picked up the frying pan of grease and threw it on him. Tawana made it clear to the officers that Jerome was only pressing charges because he was mad that Tawana had threw grease on him and Bethany had knocked the shit out of him with the umbrella stand. It was nothing more than wounded pride. The officers agreed and turned to Jerome and told him to leave the premises. They also told Bethany that if Jerome came back after they left, that she was to call the precinct and Jerome would be arrested on the spot. Apparently Jerome had made up a story when he called the cops. But once the officers got upstairs and spoke to Tawana and Bethany they found out that Jerome was lying about what happened to him. The cops figured Bethany hit him in self-defense and left it at that. The officer then walked over to Tawana and gave her a bit of advice regarding Jerome. He told Tawana to be careful because from speaking to Jerome, the officer knew Jerome was a hot-head. Tawana and Bethany tried to jump start their girls day after all the drama happened, but it was too late – the damage was done. Neither one of them was in any mood to eat. Tawana just wanted to go home, crawl up in a corner and die. She couldn't believe what this man was doing to her. Furthermore, she couldn't believe that she was allowing him to do this to her. Bethany was her best friend and Tawana did not want anything to come in between their friendship. The only real connection Tawana felt for Jerome was fear. Tawana knew that if she didn't leave Jerome she would lose not only herself, but her friends. She was not about to risk that because her and Bethany had been friends since they were snotty-nosed five year olds. Jerome simply wasn't worth it to Tawana. He was the one who had to go. It was just a matter of time.

♥

♥

CHAPTER VII

Thanks for my child

Praise him for his mighty acts: praise him
according to his excellent greatness.

Psalms 150:2

Jamal Ryan Johnson made his debut into the world on April 3, 1985. He was a delicious little thing. He weighed 7lbs. 8 oz. and was 21 inches long. He had the same chinky eyes as his mommy's. He also had her caramel brown complexion. After the delivery, Tawana was wheeled into the recovery room. There she would see Jerome standing next to a pile of coffee cups he had accumulated while waiting for her to deliver. Jerome was grinning from ear to ear despite the fact that he had nothing to offer his child. Tawana on the other hand was in her glory with her new bundle of joy. She had spent the previous months decorating his bedroom with Mickey Mouse decorations and buying clothing for his arrival. She already knew she was having a boy from the sonogram she had taken. What she didn't know was whether or not her friends or family were giving her a baby shower. Tawana started buying things for the baby ahead of time. She wanted everything to be perfect when her little bundle of joy arrived. The night before Tawana was to take little Jamal home, Bethany had called her and told her there was no heat in her apartment. Bethany told Tawana that while she was there to collect her mail, the gas company had come trying to gain access to the meter to shut off the gas service. Although Tawana had left money at home for Jerome to pay the gas bill, he never took the money to the gas company. Tawana was in no mood to fight with Jerome, so she pretended everything was okay when Jerome and Bethany arrived at the hospital to take her and baby Jamal home. When Jerome and Bethany walked through the door Tawana was sitting on the bed just staring at her baby. She couldn't believe that this bundle of joy was hers to love. It was truly a blessing to her – the way childbirth happens. You carry this little person for nine months and then one day your whole life changes. From that day on your life becomes full of responsibility. You are no longer just responsible for yourself, but the little one that God has blessed you with. Tawana always believed that children were blessings from God and while looking down in Jamal's little face she knew that he was heaven sent. She wouldn't change this day for anything in the world. Once she got Jamal home and settled down she could then focus on making their lives better. Right now she just wanted to sit and stare at this little person who was just born, but who had already brought joy to her heart. Not long after baby Jamal had come home Jerome began to get jealous of all of the attention Tawana was giving to the baby. Tawana didn't care and she spent as much time as she could with little Jamal. As the weeks went by, Tawana realized that Jerome still wasn't looking for a job. Even if he had went back to school, at least he would have been doing something. But nothing. Jerome was doing absolutely nothing!

A few weeks after Jamal had come home Tawana was getting him dressed for his first doctor's appointment. After she settled Jamal into his car seat and began driving to the doctor's office, she began to realize that she had to step up big time if she wanted to give Jamal a good quality life. She knew that she was raising a young black man and she wanted him to have all the opportunities possible to succeed in life. She did not want him to be anything like his father. Tawana decided that when she returned from the doctor's office, she would spend the rest of the day calling colleges to see if they offered any programs she'd be interested in. She really needed to attend a school where she could go full-time and still continue to work full-time. For her going back to school to get her degree was something she had to do. Although she wasn't too keen about taking out student loans, she decided that if anyone was going to invest in her future – it would have to be her. She had never relied on anyone to do anything for her and she wasn't about to start now. If going back to school was what it would take for her to give Jamal a good life, then that's what she would do – she would take out the student loans and she would repay them. She wasn't going to sit there and make excuses for why she couldn't go back to school. She knew exactly what had to be done.

♥
♥

CHAPTER VIII

A Mind is a Terrible Thing to Waste

My people shall perish for lack of knowledge.

Hosea 4:6

A few months after Jamal was born, Tawana visited Fellowship Academy and made an appointment to take the entrance exam. This was her first step at changing their lives. Once she arrived at the school she was taken to an office and given an entrance exam. It had been a while since she'd been out of high school so some of the questions on the entrance exam caught her off guard. This did not deter Tawana. She was prepared to go all the way with school and wasn't about to let an entrance exam scare her off. By the time she arrived home, she had received a telephone call from the Administrative office notifying her that she had been accepted into the school. The wonderful woman on the other line told Tawana that she would be receiving all of her material in the mail and that classes would begin in the fall. Wow, is all Tawana could think. She really wanted to go back to school but felt as if things were happening a little too fast. Nevertheless, she prepared herself for school and began her classes in the fall as scheduled. The first few months were very hard for Tawana. She was still working full time, now attending school full time and a full time mother. She had decided long ago that if Jerome wasn't going to work outside of the home, then he'd have to help her with Jamal. She didn't like this idea because Jerome wasn't as attentive to Jamal as he should have been, but she felt paying someone else to keep Jamal was a waste of money – money that she really didn't have anyway. Tawana spent the next 2 ½ years working towards her Bachelors degree. She attended school three nights a week and most nights she was so tired when she arrived home but stayed up to complete her assignments so that she'd have the weekends to spend with Jamal. Fast forward to May, 1991 -- Tawana was applying for graduation for her Bachelors Degree. She had done it despite the fact that she wanted to give up so many times while she was in school. She didn't know where she got the strength from, but she had finished. Not only did she finish school, but she finished with honors making the Dean's list every semester.

CHAPTER IX

Aint No Stopping Her Now

Ask and it will be given to you;
seek and you will find;
knock and the door will be opened to you.

Matthew 7:7-8

The morning of her graduation, Jerome for his own selfish reasons had decided to sleep late. Tawana had her hair and nails done the night before her graduation, so she pretty much had nothing to do but pass time away until her limo arrived. She and three of her girlfriends had rented a limousine to take them to the church as a treat to themselves. They were also going on a cruise to the Caribbean in July. As excited as Tawana was about going on a cruise, she knew that the cruise was still months away. She decided instead of thinking so far ahead, she would just bask in the moment – and enjoy her accomplishment right now.

The sun was shining outside and Tawana was so excited about the events of the day. She went around the corner to the local florist and purchased some Congratulations balloons for herself. She didn't need Jerome to be happy for her. His time was winding down anyway – he just didn't know it. Jerome finally woke up about an hour before Tawana was to leave. Tawana had already dressed Jamal. Jerome and Jamal were riding to the church with Tawana's parents. At 2:00 p.m. Tawana saw the limo pull up in front of the house. She looked out the window and waved to Cassandra, one of her classmates that she was on her way downstairs. She kissed Jamal and told him how handsome he looked and that she would see him at the church. He said okay mommy and continued running around the apartment. Tawana was so excited. On her way down in the elevator she couldn't help but think how proud her parents were of her. She enjoyed learning and often thought about continuing on in school to get her Masters. As she snapped out of her thoughts, the door to the elevator opened and she walked out of the building to get into the limo with her classmates. Before she could close the door to the limo, Jerome was standing on the sidewalk with Jamal in his arms. Damn, he must've jumped down the stairs in threes she thought. "He wants to go with you", Jerome said. Tawana knew where this was going and said "Jerome he can't go with me. We have to take our seats once we arrive at the church and I won't have time to look for you to take Jamal to his seat". Jerome clearly wasn't taking no for an answer and put his foot in the door as Tawana tried to close it. Tawana did not want to cause a scene and asked Jerome rather nicely to please take Jamal back upstairs and wait for her parents to arrive to drive them to the church. Jerome wouldn't budge. By this time the limo driver was becoming agitated as he knew he had a time to be at the church but he couldn't pull off until Jerome took his foot out of the door. Tawana said very nicely to the limo driver, "would you please pull off?" The limo driver said to Tawana in a very thick accent, "Mam, I can't the gentleman has his foot in the door and I cannot pull off with his foot in the door". By now, Tawana was embarrassed. Her girlfriends began to get restless and they were running against time. In the most controlled voice she could muster, she said to the limo driver, "if you want to get paid you will drive off". The limo driver started inching out of his parking spot to pull off and at that very moment, Jerome came to his senses because he took his foot out of the door and allowed the limo driver to drive off. Tawana looked back and saw Jerome standing there holding Jamal. He was so mad that Tawana thought she saw smoke coming out of his head. Tawana didn't care. She opened the bottle of wine that was in the limo and her and her classmates began to toast each other. They had waited almost three years for this day and they were determined not to let anyone spoil it.

When the limo pulled up to the church a feeling had overcome Tawana like no other. She felt so proud to see her former classmates in their caps and gowns. She saw the professors lining up the graduates and decided she should make her way to get on line. By 4:00 p.m. all of the graduates were lined up. As they began their walk up the aisle in the church, Tawana was trying to find her family in the crowd. There were so many people in the church and she did not know where her parents and Jamal were sitting. She was so nervous walking down the aisle and not seeing her family made it even worse. That was until she walked past a young man holding a handsome little boy on his shoulders. Tawana didn't know that her parents had met up with her brother, aunt and cousin and they all came to see her graduate. They were so proud of her. They were especially proud because she was the first in the family to go to college and get a degree. Her mother couldn't stop smiling. As Tawana passed the young man holding the handsome little boy she heard a little voice say "there she is, there's my mommy". It was Jamal. The young man holding Jamal was her brother Jonathan.

Tawana began to get teary eyed. Despite Jerome's actions earlier where he showed how unhappy he was that Tawana was doing something with her life, Jamal was proud of his mommy. Tawana thought he was too young to understand what was going on and maybe he was, but he knew his mommy was doing something special. The tears began to stream down her face she couldn't understand how a child could make sense of what was happening more so than an adult. After the ceremony was over, Tawana and her family went back to her apartment to celebrate. Her aunts had prepared some finger foods, bought some wine and cheese over and they just sat around talking and laughing for a few hours after the graduation. Jerome was still in jealous mode and Tawana's mother was two seconds from letting him have it. She had witnessed his behavior and was appalled at how he was acting. This was a time to be proud of Tawana and all he could do was show his jealousy and insecurity. Maybe he knew that his days were winding down. Tawana was going for bigger and better things. Unfortunately, Jerome wasn't part of the picture that she had envisioned for herself and Jamal. That night after her family had left and she had bathed Jamal and put him to bed, she began her plan. She was leaving Jerome. She didn't know how - but she was definitely leaving him. She was no longer going to subject herself to being with someone like him. He didn't appreciate her and that was his choice. But it was her choice not to stay.

CHAPTER X

I need you now

For I know the thoughts that I think toward you, saith the Lord,
thoughts of peace, and not of evil, to give you an expected end.

Jeremiah 29:11

Tawana's friends and family did not now how badly he beat her. Unfortunately Tawana wanted to keep it that way. She wanted her secret life to remain a secret. She could've easily gotten away with hiding the abuse because her bruises were always hidden – but leaving Jerome now was not an option. Besides, she had stayed for so long, why leave now? The answer was simple. He would either kill her or she would kill him. Tawana was now literally at the end of her ropes. This man had beaten her, stolen from her –he'd done just about every cruel thing you could do to a person and she still stayed. Jerome on the other hand was becoming so desperate every time she threatened to leave him that he started doing crazy things. Once he left a message on the answering machine disguising his voice. Tawana came home one day to discover a message on the machine stating that Jerome was in the hospital and needed someone to come pick him up. When Tawana called the hospital she was told there wasn't a patient there by the name of Jerome Johnson – that there must be some mistake. A few hours later Jerome came home reeking of alcohol. Tawana asked him about the message on the machine. He lied as was his usual thing and told her he was there earlier but left because they were taking too long to treat him. Tawana could not believe her ears. "You are really as crazy as I thought you were" she said to Jerome. As soon as she went to pick up Jamal to get him ready for bed, Jerome grabbed her around the neck and began fighting her. Poor Jamal had fallen out of his mother's arms and was now on the floor watching his daddy beat his mother. "Stop it, stop it please", Jamal screamed but to no avail. Jerome was like a wild man and nothing could stop him. Tawana realized that she had to fight back or she would definitely be killed. She tried punching, kicking and even biting him, but Jerome overpowered her. She ran to the kitchen to the telephone and tried to dial 911, but Jerome was right there and grabbed the phone from her. He snatched the telephone out of the wall and cut the wire to make sure she wouldn't be able to make a call. Tawana then tried to run out the front door but Jerome was a step quicker. She grabbed Jamal and ran to the bedroom trying desperately to lock the door. Jerome was right on her trail. He grabbed Jamal from her and proceeded to beat her – he wasn't finished. He began banging her head on the parquet floors and for a moment Tawana lost consciousness. When she came to she heard Jamal crying for her to get up. Jamal was actually trying to pick his mommy up but she was too heavy for him. At that moment, as Jamal was tugging on his mother's shoulder trying to push her up, she awoke. She used all the strength she had to get up off the floor. As she was balancing herself to get on her knees, she heard Jamal scream for her to watch out. The next thing

Tawana knew Jerome had a knife to her throat. He had threatened to kill her and Jamal. Tawana could not believe this was happening. It was one thing that Jerome kept hurting her, but once he started hurting Jamal, Tawana knew she had to leave this man. Tawana began screaming in the apartment trying to get someone's attention from the outside -- and it worked. One of Jerome's friends rang the door bell because he heard the screaming. As soon as Jerome opened the door, Tawana pushed the door open, grabbed Jamal and ran out of the apartment to a neighbor's house. All she had on was her panties and bra but she did not care. As she got on the elevator to go to her neighbor Ms. Anne's house Tawana was checking herself to see where she was bleeding from. She was holding onto Jamal for dear life. He was crying, she was crying and blood was everywhere. Once she arrived at Ms. Anne's house, Tawana began to examine what Jerome had done to her. She realized that the blood was coming from her head. She had lumps in her head the size of golf balls. She tried combing her hair and as she did, chunks of her hair began coming out in the comb. Ms. Anne went to her medicine cabinet to get some things to clean Tawana up. As she began cleaning the lumps in Tawana's head, Ms. Anne could not believe what she was seeing. She looked Tawana in the eyes and told Tawana that she must leave Jerome. She explained to Tawana that if she didn't leave this man he would surely kill her and maybe Jamal too. Ms. Anne knew what she was talking about because she had been in an abusive relationship. The difference between her and Tawana she said was that she went to jail for a few years. Ms. Anne had told Tawana years ago to get rid of Jerome. Unfortunately, Tawana had to figure Jerome out for herself. By the time the cops arrived, Jerome was gone and so was Tawana's car. Jerome had taken Tawana's car keys after she ran out of the apartment. Tawana was in terrible shape and Jamal was crying uncontrollably. Tawana kept trying to explain to the officers that she needed her car to get around and get Jamal to school. The cops were discussing with each other the best possible way for them to get Jerome to bring Tawana's car back. Seeing the condition Jerome had left Tawana in, the cops wanted a piece of Jerome. They wanted to kick his natural black ass. Unfortunately, no matter how Tawana looked, there was a system that had to be followed. The cops had to fill out a domestic violence report and then Tawana would have to go to the hospital to have herself checked out. As the cops were finishing up their report, they gave Tawana a few telephone numbers to shelters just in case she needed to go to one – at least for that night. The officers had spoken with Jerome's cousin, Jonah, and Jonah was to meet them at the police station with Tawana's car. Tawana told the officers that she just needed her car back first, they could arrest Jerome after his cousin drove it safely to the precinct. At about 2:00 in the morning, the telephone rang. Tawana was afraid to answer the call but she did anyway. It was the officers telling her that her car was at the precinct and that she could pick it up anytime. Tawana thanked them and told them that she would be there sometime in the late afternoon. She had to go to the hospital first to have herself checked out. After her conversation with the officers, Tawana laid down and her mind just started wandering. She could not understand how her life had gotten to this point. She felt totally helpless and this was not a good feeling to her. One thing she knew for sure was that it was over. No matter what she was trying to hold on to, she had to leave Jerome. He had lost all hope after Tawana told him she no longer wanted to be with him. He became desperate. Tawana also knew that this situation was having a terrible effect on Jamal. He was old enough to understand what he had seen as he had begun acting out in school. All night instead of going to sleep he wanted to know when his daddy was coming home. If it were up to Tawana his daddy would've been buried under the nearest jail, but it wasn't. The next morning when Tawana awoke, she prepared herself to do something that she never wanted to do. She got Jamal washed and dressed and she went to the hospital. From the moment she stepped into the emergency room, she became a statistic. She'd spent the last 10 years of her life trying to avoid becoming a number, but this was something she couldn't avoid. She was there seeking treatment for her latest beating at the hands of Jerome. She filled out the necessary papers for the triage nurse and was told to have a seat until her name was called. Half an hour later Tawana was called. Bethany had just walked into the emergency room. She kissed Tawana and told Tawana to go on, that she would take care of Jamal. Tawana walked into the triage room, handed the nurse her paperwork and saw what looked like a camera in the nurse's hand. With the flashbulbs flashing, she heard the nurse bark out her orders "turn to the left" please, "turn to the right please". The nurse was taking pictures of her bruises. These bruises could not be hidden and that it was compelled Tawana to finally do something about the abuse. The lie was over. Her friends knew what was going on, her mother knew and her family knew. Her secret was out. Everyone stood in the background wondering what Tawana would do next. They all knew she was a smart young lady but sometimes love can make you do dumb things. Tawana had enough – this was the last straw. From this day on, her life was about to change in a good way. She began praying like she'd never prayed before. Praying for God to deliver her from this mess of a relationship. Praying for God to help her see her way out of it. Most of all she prayed that she would live to raise Jamal. That was her greatest fear, that one day Jerome would really lose it and literally beat her to death. She was not going to let that happen so she began to plot her escape. It was well over two years since her graduation and she was still with Jerome. Fear of the unknown is paralyzing. Tawana was definitely afraid of what Jerome could do to her and Jamal – especially since he knew his days were numbered.

♥

♥

CHAPTER XI

Through Christ I can do all things

Yea, though I walk through the valley of the shadow of death,
I will fear no evil: for thou art with me;
thy rod and thy staff they comfort me.

Psalms **23:4**

A few months had passed since Tawana's visit to the hospital. Against the advice of her friends and family, Tawana had let Jerome move back in her apartment. She told Jerome what she expected of him and since he really had no place to go, he agreed to do whatever Tawana said. What he didn't know was that Tawana had a plan. She had been praying for strength to leave Jerome. It seemed like an eternity that she was praying. She lie in bed one night and schemed up a plan to get Jerome out of her life. As bad as she wanted him out of her life, she also wanted to be alive to take care of Jamal. After the way Jerome fought her the last time sending her to the hospital, Tawana had to be very careful. She called her parents and told them that she wanted to come stay with them until she could figure out what to do next. It had been years since Tawana and her siblings had left home and her parents were excited at the thought of having Jamal there with them. Jamal had grown up so nicely and was a little man, his grandma and grandpa just loved showering him with toys and hugs and kisses. Tawana had decided that she would wait until the school year was over before she and Jamal moved in with her parents. While speaking with her mother a few weeks before the move, Ms. Janie asked Tawana what would happen to Jerome once she and Jamal moved in with her. Tawana told her mother that she really did not care where Jerome went. She told her mother that Jerome had done so many cruel things to her over the course of their relationship that she didn't care about what happened to him. Ms. Janie did not like to hear Tawana talk this way, especially since Tawana had been helping people all of her life. Ms. Janie told Tawana not to let this man change who she was because then she was giving him power over her. Tawana understood what her mother was saying but she knew it would take prayer and therapy to change the way she felt about Jerome. Ms. Janie suggested that Tawana let Jerome move in with them until he could get on his feet. Tawana wanted to tell her mother that Jerome had been trying to get on his feet since they met and he still had not landed on them. Tawana was tired of waiting. The wait was officially over. Although Tawana did not want Jerome to come she began to realize how perfectly this would fit into her plan. Tawana knew that Jerome would not put a hand on her as long as he was in her parents' home. It all began to make sense to her. For sure Jerome would be on his best behavior and Tawana could finally get rid of him without a problem. The morning of the move, Tawana picked up the moving truck because Jerome was sleeping. When she got back home, she began loading the truck with the belongings that she intended to keep. Everything else, she either gave away or threw away. The truck was completely loaded by 4:00 p.m. and they were on their way. When they reached her parents home, Tawana was excited to see that her parents were sitting on the porch patiently awaiting their arrival.

It was only a few months after moving in with her parents and now Jerome was driving Tawana crazy. She despised him. She couldn't stand looking at him. To make matters worse, he was taking his sweet time trying to find a place to stay. Although she knew she no longer loved him and did not want to be with him, she was afraid of what he was capable of doing to her and Jamal. She never told anyone what her plans were with regard to Jerome. She just continued to pray day in and day out that someday he would be a distant memory in her life and she could finally move on.

That day came sooner than she thought it would when one sunny morning in September, Tawana was awaken by a bright stream of sun emanating into the basement. Tawana thought this to be very weird since basements usually don't have much sun – especially not the way she saw it on this day. As she made her way to the bathroom to wash her face and brush her teeth, Tawana felt a surge of power go through her body. She couldn't explain this feeling, but she knew it was like no other feeling she had felt before. At that moment she thought she was going crazy. What was going on she thought. She started thinking about how she had been praying and asking God to help her get out of her situation and realized that the feeling that she had experienced was God. Tawana couldn't believe it. She knew that God always answered her prayers but she had been praying for so long that she began to think God did not hear her. She thought back to the old woman she had met years earlier in church who had told her that God is an "on-time" God. He doesn't do things when we want him to, but when he's ready to. The old woman had told Tawana that when you are at your worst going through things, God is at his best, making a way for you. It all became clear to Tawana now. Today was her day of redemption. She went into the bathroom, washed her face and brushed her teeth. When she came out of the bathroom, she walked over to Jerome's side of the bed and tapped Jerome on the shoulder. Jerome opened his eyes, looked up at Tawana and said "what's wrong, why are you up so early"? Tawana told Jerome that he had to leave. She went on to tell him how she did not love him (which probably was the umpteenth time that she told him that) and that today was the day that she was changing her life without him. Jerome sat up with a puzzled look on his face. He wondered what he had done wrong. Tawana looked at him and said "you just don't get it Jerome do you? I told you before we moved in with my parents that you would have to find a place to live but you kept prolonging it as if I would change my mind". Jerome looked sad, and usually his sad look would work on Tawana – but not today. Today was her day of redemption for all of those years of turmoil. She was not about to let Jerome's sad face change her plans. She knew how he could be Jekyll and Hyde and she wasn't about to fall for it – not this time. "Ok, said Jerome, if you don't want me then I'm going to leave, but I have to save some money before I start looking for a place". Tawana would hear none of that. She told Jerome that she would begin calling landlord's trying to get him a place to stay. Jerome looked betrayed when Tawana said this. But Tawana really didn't care. Payback was a mother she thought. All the times she cried herself to sleep after his beatings, she had no remorse for him at all. She had been waiting for this day for years and she wasn't about to let a sad face change her mind.

♥
♥

CHAPTER XII

Ain't No Sunshine Until He's Gone

In the day when I cried thou answered me,
and strengthened me with strength in my soul.

Psalms 138:3

Tawana and Jamal were settling into their new digs. They had the entire basement and Tawana decorated it as it if were a full apartment. She had much more space in her apartment, but right now she had to make due with what she had. She had peace of mind here at her parents' home, something she could never get at her own apartment. Jerome on the other hand could not get used to his surroundings. He felt uncomfortable. Probably because his secret was out. Everyone now knew that he was beating Tawana for years. He had no place to go so he had to deal with it. The plan was that he would only go with Tawana and Jamal until he found something of his own. Tawana had grown tired of him delaying his move after all they had moved in with her parents in July. By October she began pressuring him to find a room. One day she came home from work and he was crying about how he didn't have anywhere to go and no money. Tawana had a long day at work and really wasn't in a mood to hear Jerome's whining. She knew what she had to do when she got to work the next day. If he wouldn't look for a place to live she'd have to do it for him. Tawana began looking for a room for Jerome. He wasn't making any attempt and Tawana could not stand to look at him anymore. He was so weak to her. She really couldn't understand how she could still be with him. Every Sunday she would purchase the local paper and look through it with the hopes that she would find a place for Jerome to live. She wrote down a few numbers and began calling the landlord's to see if the rooms were available and what the rental fee was. She had spoken with six potential landlords, unfortunately, she could not afford what they were asking for. Before she got to the last number, Tawana got lucky. The landlord on the other end of the phone told Tawana what her rental fee was, how she wanted her rent to be paid and a few other rules she spewed off to Tawana. All Tawana heard was the rental fee and when the rent was due. Everything else did not apply to her since she was not the one who would be actually renting the room.

Tawana couldn't wait to tell Jerome the good news. Well at least it was good news to her. All her hard work had paid off. When Tawana told Jerome he pretended to be excited about the news although the look on his face said something else.

Tomorrow Tawana would stop by her bank and withdraw $600 from her savings account. This was the last $600 she had and although she knew she had to replenish the funds she was taking out, she couldn't help but think what good use she was putting the funds to. In her mind, she was paying for her freedom. She met Jerome that evening and they rode over to the landlord's house. The landlord showed them the room,

Jerome signed a monthly lease, gave her the money and she gave him his keys and his receipt. When they arrived back at Tawana's parents home, Tawana helped Jerome pack his belongings. She placed his things in the garage so that when it was time to go she could simply load them into her car. Tomorrow would be a new day for her and Jamal. Tawana couldn't wait. It seemed as if she waited for this day her entire life and it had finally come. She remembers when she used to sit around and hope something happened to Jerome so he could be out of her life. She knew thinking that way was not right but Jerome had done so much wrong to her that she couldn't help feeling this way. All she knew was she wanted Jerome out of her life for good.

As the sun was rising, Tawana began to awake...this was the day. Tawana was ready to rock and roll. She had her car loaded already with Jerome's belongings. She was just waiting for Jerome to wake up and get himself ready. Of course, Jerome slept later than usual, but Tawana wasn't worried. For the first time in her life, she had taken control and it felt good. She had told herself that she would never allow someone to wreak so much havoc in her life again – allowing her to feel powerless. Tawana had learned a valuable lesson from her relationship with Jerome. She had given this man ten years of her life. Ten years that she would never get back. The best thing that came out of those ten years was her precious Jamal. Tawana had so much making up to do with Jamal. There were many nights that she was so stressed from Jerome that she didn't spend quality time with Jamal. She was truly sorry for this, but she knew that times were about to change and things were about to change. Their lives would now be free of controversy and Tawana couldn't wait.

♥
♥

Yes, its Over

Faith is the substance of things hoped for,
the evidence of things not seen.

Hebrews 11:1

The drive home after dropping Jerome off Tawana's shoulders were so light. The day had come. She was finally rid of Jerome and she didn't know whether she wanted to laugh or cry. She began to think about how their relationship had started out and realized that it was not a good one from the beginning. She wished she had left Jerome earlier than she did. But she realized that although her experience with him wasn't a good one, she had learned a valuable lesson. She always knew that God would deliver her out of the relationship, but at times, she still became weary. Through it all she had learned that there were some things that people couldn't teach you -- you only learned them through life experiences. She had heard the saying many times that experience is your best teacher and she believed that. She learned that all the things that Jerome had done to her he only did because she allowed him to. All those years of being afraid of him had paralyzed her terribly. Jerome knew she was afraid and he used that to his advantage to further intimidate her. She was stopped at the red light and she began to daydream about her life, what she'd been through and where she wanted to go. She looked in her rear view mirror and looked at Jamal sleeping without a care in the world. She was determined that his life would be just that – without a care in the world. She would take care of everything for Jamal. There would be no limits. She already had her Bachelors degree but now she wanted more. She wanted to make sure that life would be good for her and Jamal. She knew this wasn't possible unless she got a better education. She would go back to school for her Masters. Tawana felt like she could conquer the world. She thought back to her high school days and what she had written in her high school yearbook under her picture. She had written "the world is yours" and that is exactly how she felt. Her possibilities for a happy, productive life were endless. She would continue working and going to school all the while making a better life for her and Jamal. The world was hers... and she was going after it – and this time, nobody was going to stop her!

About the Author

The author is a native New Yorker currently residing in Newburgh, New York. She is married and has two children. Mrs. Jones has a Masters of Administration and Bachelors of Professional Studies from Manhattan Community College of New York where she graduated Summa Cum Laude. She has spent time volunteering with teens, the elderly and at soup kitchens throughout the city.

www.ingramcontent.com/pod-product-compliance
Lightning Source LLC
Chambersburg PA
CBHW021258280526
45784CB00005B/2416